ISBN: 978-1-7321173-6-5 (Paperback)

Front cover image & book artwork by Toby Mikle.

First printing edition 2018.

Son & Reign Publishers
PO Box 2940
San Francisco, CA 94126

PaulDeannoBooks.com

To My Mom: Thank you for your
constant love and support!

Winter is here, and I want you to know,

My **favorite** time of the year is when it starts to **SNOW!**

Millions of snowflakes falling from the sky,
When a big storm comes it can pile 3 FEET HIGH!

If a snowstorm hits your town, I'd say you're in luck.
But did you know... sitting on your roof...
It can be as heavy as **TWO CARS & A TRUCK!!!**

Just one foot of wet snow on a roof
can weigh up to 12,000 pounds!

When it starts getting cold, it's time for snow,
Time to get outside & have some fun.
It snows in all 50 states,
That's right – **EVERY SINGLE ONE!**
You may be wondering about one place,
A state that's famous for being warm.
But there's a really TALL mountain in Hawaii,
And the very top can get a winter storm.

Hawaii is a great place to visit... if you want to go to

The Beach.

But just like every other state in winter,
SNOW isn't that far out of reach.

It snows almost every winter on Hawaii's two
tallest mountains: Mauna Kea & Mauna Loa

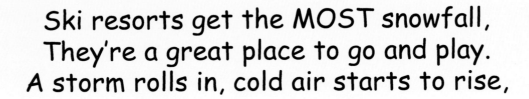

Ski resorts get the MOST snowfall,
They're a great place to go and play.
A storm rolls in, cold air starts to rise,

& It can snow ALL DAY!

There's one place with the most snowfall,
A mountain in the Pacific Northwest.
It's called **Mount Baker**, and in the record
books, it's snow rises above the rest.

Mt. Baker received 1140" snow in the 1998-1999 winter season.

In just one winter, it dumped **95 FEET**,
More than a thousand inches of snow.
That's as high as three T-Rex's AND a giraffe,
With five more feet to go!

When the weatherman says, "Get ready!
It's going to snow **TODAY!**",
Have you ever wondered how it got here,
It may have traveled a long way.

There's something called the "**JET STREAM**",
A super-fast, super-high current of air.
It's kind of like train tracks up in the sky,
Carrying storms from here to there.

In wintertime the jet stream
Stretches from coast to coast.
Where it will go is where it will **SNOW**,
Maybe at YOUR house it'll snow the MOST!!!

Winds inside the polar jet stream
can be 200 mph or stronger!

Snow falls when it's **COLD** outside and there's a storm,
But some animals actually use the snow to try and

Stay real **WARM!**

They dig a hole that's not too big
& surrounded by the snow.

The animal's body heat gets trapped inside,
& the temperature doesn't get too low.

How does that happen? The snow is an "insulator",
Keeping the warm air in place.
So it may super windy and cold outside,
But **UNDER THE SNOW** it's a much warmer space.

10 inches of fresh snow can trap heat
as well as 6" of fiberglass insulation.

When a fresh snow falls,
And you walk on your street.
Counting every single snowflake
Would be an **IMPOSSIBLE** feat.
There are thousands of snowflakes
In just one snowman's head.
And **MILLIONS** more in the tracks
Of your best friend's new sled.

Each and every snowflake is **DIFFERENT**, that's true,

You'll never find two exactly alike...
They're ALL unique – **JUST LIKE YOU!**

There are 35 main shapes of snowflakes, but each one
is just a little different in size and structure.

If you LOVE winter, you LOVE snow, that's for sure!
And there are some ways Mother Nature makes it snow

EVEN MORE!

A storm so STRONG it has lightning is one way,
The snow falls really hard & the name is fun to say:

"THUNDERSNOW!"

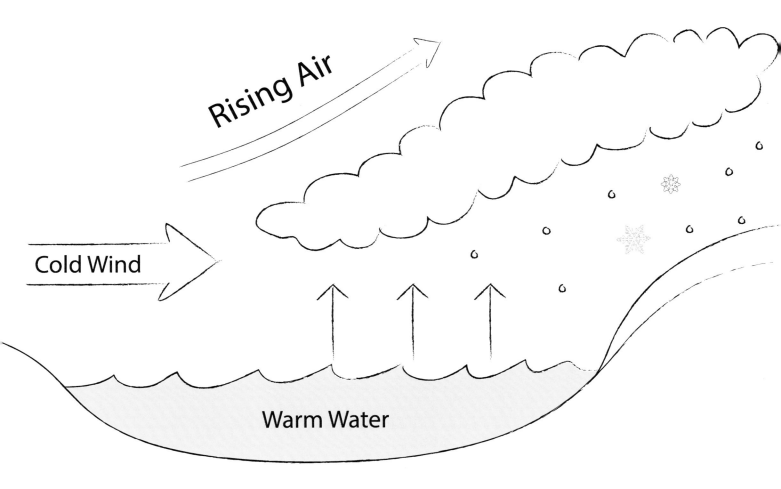

In other places, cold air moves over a warm lake,
And where that wind blows, snowfall records may break!

It snowed 49" in just ONE DAY in Watertown,
NY, due to a "lake-effect" snowstorm!

So many fun things to do when snow starts to fall,
You can slide, you can sled, or make a

REALLY BIG snowball!

It's important to know not all snow is the same,
DRY snow is great for skiing,
But makes a snowball fight a very hard game.

If you can, find some snow that's been sitting in the Sun.

That'll make it **WETTER**, and much better,
For some snowball making fun!

The world's biggest snowball fight happened in Canada in 2016. More than 7600 people took part!

We **LOVE** the snow in winter,
But did you ever think...

When spring comes, the snow will melt,
And turn into **WATER** that we drink!

It's kind of cool to see what starts as one snowflake,
Becomes a drop of water in a stream, a river,

& then a lake.

So imagine this: It's January,
and when it's snowing real hard.

In June, that water will help a
BEAUTIFUL FLOWER grow in your yard!

On average, 10 inches of snow will
melt into 1 inch of liquid water.

To Read Paul's
"Weather 'Whys' For Kids" Blog,
Visit His Website:

PaulDeannoBooks.com

Connect With Paul & "WOW! Weather" On Social Media

- FACEBOOK -- WOW Weather
- TWITTER -- @WowWeather_Book
- TWITTER -- @PaulKPIX
- INSTAGRAM -- @BayAreaWxGuy

Other "WOW! Weather!" Titles

The End

About the Author

Paul Deanno has won five Emmy Awards for his work as a broadcast meteorologist in some of the largest television markets in the country. He is also the first meteorologist to do the weather on all three network morning newscasts: Good Morning America (ABC), The Today Show (NBC), and CBS This Morning. Paul lives in the San Francisco Bay Area with his beautiful wife, Suzanne, and their three boys.

Made in the USA
San Bernardino, CA
03 March 2019